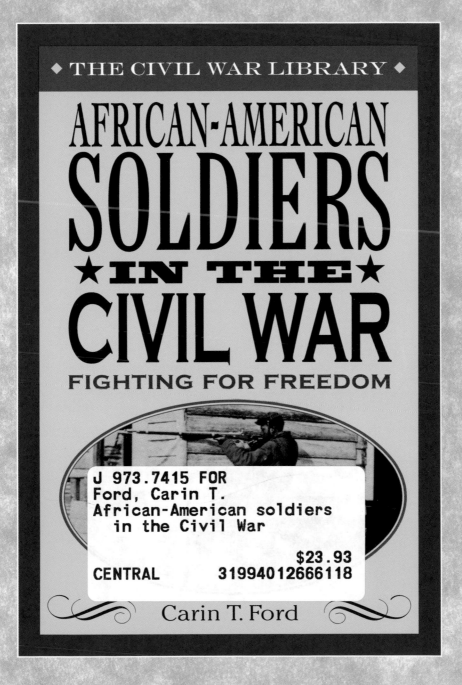

♦ THE CIVIL WAR LIBRARY ♦

AFRICAN-AMERICAN
SOLDIERS
★ IN THE ★
CIVIL WAR
FIGHTING FOR FREEDOM

Carin T. Ford

Enslow Publishers, Inc.
40 Industrial Road   PO Box 38
Box 398   Aldershot
Berkeley Heights, NJ 07922   Hants GU12 6BP
USA   UK

http://www.enslow.com

Library of Congress Cataloging-in-Publication Data

Ford, Carin T.
 African-American soldiers in the Civil War : fighting for freedom /
 Carin T. Ford.
  v. cm. — (The Civil War library)
 Includes bibliographical references and index.
 Contents: A new country — The way is barred — Recruitment — The first regiments — Separate but unequal — Timeline.
  ISBN 0-7660-2254-4 (hardcover)
 1. United States—History—Civil War, 1861–1865—Participation, African American—Juvenile literature. 2. African American soldiers—History—19th century—Juvenile literature. [1. African American soldiers—History—19th century. 2. United States—History—Civil War, 1861–1865—Participation, African American. 3. Race relations—History.] I. Title.
 E540.N3F675 2004
 973.7'415—dc22   2003013724

Printed in the United States of America

10 9 8 7 6 5 4 3 2 1

To Our Readers: We have done our best to make sure all Internet Addresses in this book were active and appropriate when we went to press. However, the author and the publisher have no control over and assume no liability for the material available on those Internet sites or on other Web sites they may link to. Any comments or suggestions can be sent by e-mail to comments@enslow.com or to the address on the back cover.

Every effort has been made to locate all copyright holders of material used in this book. If any errors or omissions have occurred, corrections will be made in future editions of this book.

Illustration Credits: © Bettmann/Corbis, p. 9; *The Black Phalanx*, Hartford: American Publishing Co., 1888, p. 15; Boston Athenaeum, p. 6B; Collection of The New-York Historical Society, negative number 45301, pp. 1, 16; Collection of The New-York Historical Society, PR-055-3-60, pp. 20, 42 (poster); Collection of The New-York Historical Society, PR-055-3-15, p. 21TL; Collection of The New-York Historical Society, PR-065-815-7, pp. 33 (inset), 36; Department of Defense, p. 38T; Dover Publications, Inc., pp. 2, 7R, 21BR, 23T, 26, 28B, 37B, 43TR; Enslow Publishers, Inc., p. 11; Library of Congress, pp. 4–5, 5 (inset), 6T, 7L, 10, 13 (inset), 14B, 17B, 18 (inset), 19, 22–23B, 25 (inset), 28T, 30T, 30–31C, 31R, 33 (background), 35, 37T, 38B, 40T, 41, 42CL, 43BL, 43TL; Photographs and Prints Division, Schomburg Center for Research in Black Culture, The New York Public Library, Astor, Lenox and Tilden Foundations, pp. 13 (background), 17T, 18 (background), 20T, 24T, 24B, 25 (background), 27, 29, 32T, 32B, 34, 42TR, 42BC; Missouri Historical Society, St. Louis, by Thomas Satterwhite Noble, p. 8; National Archives and Records Administration, pp. 12, 14T, 21BL, 39, 40B, 43BR.

Cover Illustration: *Inset*, Collection of The New-York Historical Society, negative number 45301; All cover photos courtesy of the following: Library of Congress; National Archives; Photos.com; Enslow Publishers, Inc.; with the exception of: Song Book, Courtesy National Park Service, Museum Management Program and Gettysburg National Military Park, catalog number GETT31374, www.cr.nps.gov/museum/exhibits/gettex/music2.htm; Patriotic Cover, Courtesy National Park Service, Museum Management Program and Gettysburg National Military Park, catalog number GETT27703, www.cr.nps.gov/museum/exhibits/gettex/write5.htm; Drum carried by Mozart Regiment, Courtesy National Park Service, Museum Management Program and Gettysburg National Military Park, catalog number GETT32847, www.cr.nps.gov/museum/exhibits/gettex/music3.htm; US Flag, Courtesy National Park Service, Museum Management Program and Manassas National Battlefield Park, catalog number MANA979, www.cr.nps.gov/museum/exhibits/flags/mana2.htm.

TABLE OF CONTENTS

CHAPTER ONE

A NEW COUNTRY

Six hundred Union soldiers raced toward Fort Wagner in South Carolina. The men were wet, tired, and hungry. It was July 1863, and the Fifty-fourth Massachusetts Regiment was one of the first units of African-American soldiers fighting in the Civil War. One soldier carried the Union flag, showing that the men were

Black soldiers showed their loyalty and courage when they stormed Fort Wagner in 1863.

fighting for the North. Colonel Robert Gould Shaw had told his soldiers to "take the fort or die there."[1] The men promised to try. Yet, inside the fort, nearly three times as many Confederate soldiers were waiting with guns and cannons.

Robert Gould Shaw came from a family that was strongly against slavery. He agreed to command an all-black troop, saying he wanted "to prove that a Negro can be made a good soldier."[2]

Bullets flew and the Union soldiers fell, one after another. The soldier holding the Union flag was shot. Quickly, Sergeant William H. Carney reached out and grabbed the flag. As the regiment was ordered back to camp, Carney ran through a storm of bullets. He was shot in the head, chest, arm, and leg—but he did not let go of the flag.

"The old flag never touched the ground," Carney said proudly when he was safely back at camp with his unit.[3]

William H. Carney became the first African American to receive the Congressional Medal of Honor. It was awarded for his bravery at Fort Wagner.

The charge on Fort Wagner was a defeat for the North. The regiment lost almost half of its men, including Colonel Robert Shaw. But the soldiers of the Fifty-fourth did not feel defeated. They had shown their courage. They had proved that black men could be soldiers.

❖ The North was also known as the Union, or the United States. The people there were often called Yankees.

❖ The South was called the Confederacy, or the Confederate States. During the war, Southerners were also called Rebels or Johnny Reb.

When the Civil War broke out in April 1861, very few people thought African Americans should be allowed to fight. It was called a white man's war, meaning it was up to whites to serve in the army and navy.[4] Yet the war had everything to do with black Americans.

There had been slavery in the United States for nearly 250 years. It had begun when a Dutch ship brought twenty African slaves to Virginia in 1619. By the outbreak of the Civil War, there were close to 4 million slaves in the country. These people had no rights. They were bought and sold like property. Many slaves were torn away from their families, beaten, whipped, and half-starved.

Most slaves lived in the South. Tobacco, rice, sugarcane, and cotton grew well there. The slaves worked from sunrise to sunset planting, plowing, and harvesting the crops. After the cotton gin was invented in 1793, the demand for slaves skyrocketed. The cotton gin was a machine that removed the seeds from the cotton. Fifty times more cotton could be cleaned each day—and farmers could make even more money selling cotton. On their huge plantations, Southern farmers used slaves to produce nearly two-thirds of all the cotton grown in the world.

People in the United States had different opinions about slavery. Most Southerners believed they needed slaves to grow cotton. In the North, the businesses and small farms did not depend on slave labor. Many Northerners began to say that it was wrong for one person to own another person.

By the 1860s, many people in the North believed that slavery was cruel. Slaves worked long hours and were often treated harshly by their owners.

9

In November 1860, Abraham Lincoln was elected president. By then, one out of every seven Americans was a slave.[5] Lincoln had often spoken out against slavery. As president, would he put an end to slavery?

People in the South were worried. They did not think the government in Washington, D.C., had the right to tell them what to do about slavery. Southerners said each state should decide for itself.

South Carolina seceded—or broke away—from the rest of the country in December 1860. Soon, six more Southern states followed: Mississippi, Florida, Alabama, Georgia, Louisiana, and Texas. Together, they formed a new country. They called it the Confederate States of America.

On April 12, 1861, Confederate soldiers fired on Fort Sumter in South Carolina. The United States soldiers surrendered the fort to the

The shots fired on Fort Sumter in Charleston, South Carolina, marked the start of the Civil War.

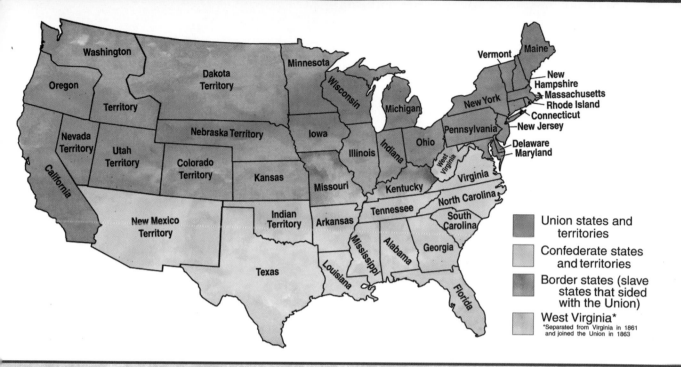

Washington	
Oregon	
Territory	Dakota Territory
Nevada Territory	
Utah Territory	Nebraska Territory
California	Colorado Territory
New Mexico Territory	Kansas
	Indian Territory
	Texas

Minnesota · Wisconsin · Michigan · Iowa · Illinois · Indiana · Ohio · Missouri · Kentucky · Tennessee · Arkansas · Mississippi · Louisiana · Alabama · Georgia · Florida · South Carolina · North Carolina · Virginia · West Virginia · Vermont · Maine · New Hampshire · Massachusetts · Rhode Island · Connecticut · New Jersey · New York · Pennsylvania · Delaware · Maryland

Union states and territories

Confederate states and territories

Border states (slave states that sided with the Union)

West Virginia*
*Separated from Virginia in 1861 and joined the Union in 1863

Confederates. The North and the South were at war. After that, four more slave states joined the Confederacy: Virginia, Arkansas, Tennessee, and North Carolina.

President Lincoln called for 75,000 volunteers to serve in the Union army and fight for the United States of America. He said he would not allow the nation to be split in two. The Civil War began as a fight to put the country back together. But African Americans hoped that a war between North and South would also put an end to slavery—and they wanted to take part in it.

Former slave Frederick Douglass urged African Americans to join the war.

Frederick Douglass was an ex-slave who became famous as a speaker and writer against slavery. He told African-American men and women to fight for their freedom. "I urge you to fly to arms," Douglass said. "This is your golden opportunity."[6]

Still, the United States War Department continued to turn away African Americans. Many white Northerners thought slavery was wrong, but they did not think black people were equal to whites. They did not want to fight side by side with black soldiers.

Besides, most Northerners were certain the Civil War would be over in a few months. The Union had more factories, more guns, and more men than the Confederacy. The Union army said it did not need any help from African Americans.

"Let us do something . . . ," Douglass urged the government. "We are ready and would go."[7] But when African Americans asked to help fight the war, the door was closed to them.

CHAPTER TWO

THE WAY IS BARRED

A law from the late 1700s said that blacks could not fight in the United States Army. Yet, early in the Civil War, a few army officials tried to put together units of African-American soldiers. When the government would not supply them with guns, uniforms, or money, these units fell apart.

Major General David Hunter believed that African Americans could help the North win the war.[1] In May 1862, he put together a unit of black soldiers. But President Lincoln and the War Department ordered him to disband his men.

As the Civil War dragged on, many slaves escaped from their plantations and headed for Union army camps. Some Union officers sent the slaves back to their masters. But often slaves were allowed to stay with the soldiers. They were called "contraband of war." This meant they were like goods taken from the enemy. Now they belonged to the North.

The contrabands helped in any way they could. Men drove wagons, dug trenches for the soldiers, and worked as cooks and servants. Women did laundry, sewing, housekeeping, and nursing. Some were spies and scouts.

◆ ONE CONTRABAND'S STORY ◆

Mary Ann Cox was a slave on a cotton plantation. Her first husband had been sold to another slave owner, and her second husband had died. In July 1863, Mary Ann ran away with her son, Everett. They joined a contraband camp in Tennessee.

When Everett joined the Union army, Mary Ann traveled with the regiment as a washerwoman. After a fierce battle in Mississippi, Mary Ann waited for her son to return to camp. But Everett had been captured and later died in an Alabama prison.[2]

It was clear by the middle of 1862 that the war was not going to end quickly. More than twenty battles had already been fought. The number of wounded and dead soldiers was growing. At the same time, the number of white volunteer soldiers was dropping. The Union army needed more men.

In July 1862, the United States Congress gave President

SLAVES FIGHT?

 Most slaves in the South were loyal to their masters at the start of the war. But after the Emancipation Proclamation, many slaves learned

that they had the chance to be free. Thousands of slaves ran away to join the Union army.[4]

Lincoln the power to hire African-American soldiers.[3] He ordered Secretary of War Edwin Stanton to recruit black soldiers in the Sea Islands near South Carolina.

On January 1, 1863, Lincoln issued the Emancipation Proclamation. It stated that all slaves in the rebelling states were now free.

Southerners did not set their slaves free just because Lincoln told them to. Lincoln had no power in the Confederate states. Still, the South lost many slaves as Union soldiers swept through to recruit men. The soldiers promised freedom to any male slave who joined the Union army.

Many black soldiers were eager to go to battle. The soldiers shown here were on guard duty.

The Emancipation Proclamation changed the reason for the Civil War. The war was no longer just about putting the country back together. Now soldiers were also fighting to put an end to slavery.

Contraband workers headed off for the day with shovels, picks, and other tools.

CHAPTER THREE

RECRUITMENT

Once African Americans learned that they could serve in the army and the navy, they quickly started signing up. One man in New Orleans said that he would "fight as long as I can. If only my boy may stand in the street equal to a white boy when the war is over."[1]

Many of the new soldiers came from the

North, where African-American businessmen and ministers urged men to join. They gave speeches, held meetings, and handed out flyers. Black soldiers were also telling other African Americans to enlist. "Let us make a name for ourselves and race," said one soldier at a meeting in Nashville, Tennessee.[2]

Special posters were made to recruit African Americans.

From the start, Lincoln knew that there would have to be separate units for the African-American soldiers.

COME AND JOIN US BROTHERS.
PUBLISHED BY THE SUPERVISORY COMMITTEE FOR RECRUITING COLORED REGIMENTS

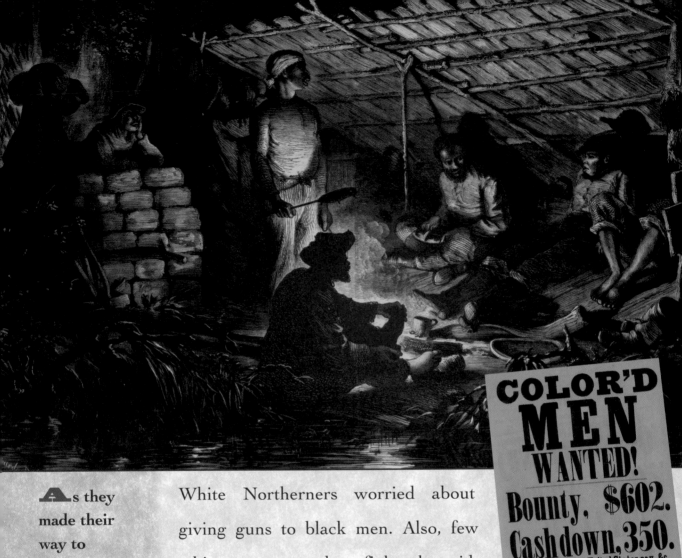

COLOR'D MEN WANTED! Bounty, $602. Cash down, 350. Besides State, and United States pay, &c.

Recruits will be mustered into Colored Regiments.

APPLY TO JAMES S. HENRY; At Recruiting Office, Second & Bridge Ave.

Camden, Dec. 23d, 1863.

As they made their way to the North, runaway slaves hid from slave catchers.

White Northerners worried about giving guns to black men. Also, few white men wanted to fight alongside black soldiers.

Flyers calling for men to join the Union army had two separate messages: one for whites, the other for blacks. Black men were told to prove that they could be good soldiers. Whites were told that the army needed more

ATTENTION!
$727 TO VETERANS,
$627 for all White Men
Who Volunteer to fill the old N. J. Regiments.
$400 CASH,
When Mustered into the United States Service.
If you are drafted you get no BOUNTY. Apply to
JOHN D. SMALLWOOD,
PARSON'S HOTEL, CAMDEN, N. J.
December 11, 1863.

men—and that was why blacks were being asked to join.

Nearly all the officers in charge of the black units were white. The public, and the army, had a hard enough time with the idea of African-American soldiers. Lincoln believed that they would never accept African-American officers.

When Union soldiers came to Southern plantations, thousands of slaves risked punishment, and even death, by running away to become soldiers. The slave owners did not give up easily. Runaways who were caught were often beaten or shot dead. Two slaves had their left ears cut off when they were found trying to enlist. But for slaves, the chance to be free was worth any risk.

TO COLORED MEN!
FREEDOM,
Protection, Pay, and a Call to Military Duty!

WHEN SLAVES RAN AWAY

❖ Slave owners were furious when they learned that any of their slaves had run away to join the Union army. They often punished the slave's family. A slave in Missouri begged her husband to come home. She wrote that she had been beaten "most cruelly" with a leather strap because her husband had enlisted in the army.[3]

Elijah Marrs was a Kentucky slave who ran away to join the army. Twenty-seven other slaves went with him. In late September 1864, Marrs led the men to Louisville. They traveled at night, hiding in ditches to keep from being caught. At last the men reached the army's recruiting office.

"I felt freedom in my bones," Marrs said. When he saw the American flag, all his fears disappeared.[4]

Marrs became a sergeant in the Twelfth U.S. Colored Heavy Artillery.

Runaway slaves too young to fight were still able to help the Union army. After George Ellis escaped from slavery, he worked as a servant to an officer. In 1865, when Ellis was old enough to join the army, he joined the Fifty-fifth Massachusetts Colored Infantry.

Men of the 107th U.S. Colored Infantry posed with their musical instruments.

23

It was not easy for a black man to become a soldier. Yet by the end of the war, one out of every eight soldiers in the Union army was African American.[5] For most, wearing the army uniform was a source of great pride.

"This was the biggest thing that ever happened in my life," said a former slave. "I felt like a man with a uniform on and a gun in my hand."[6]

During four years of war, nearly 100,000 blacks from the Confederate states joined the Union army. About 45,000 ex-slaves or free men joined from the border states. Another 50,000 or more came from the Northern states and the Colorado Territory.

This man escaped from slavery (top) and became a Union soldier (right).

CHAPTER FOUR

THE FIRST REGIMENTS

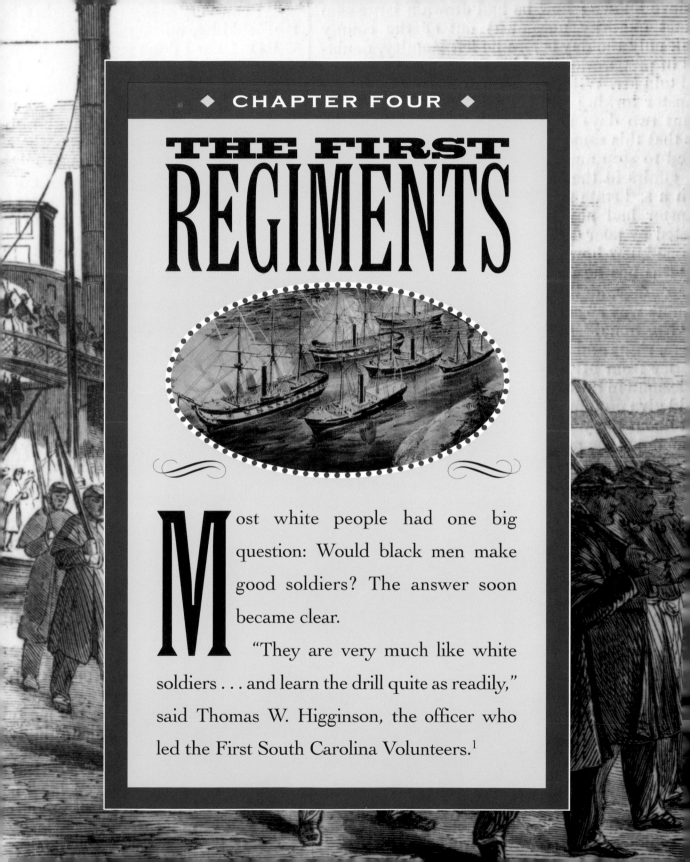

Most white people had one big question: Would black men make good soldiers? The answer soon became clear.

"They are very much like white soldiers . . . and learn the drill quite as readily," said Thomas W. Higginson, the officer who led the First South Carolina Volunteers.[1]

Cavalry soldiers, below, were trained to fight on horseback. Many whites doubted that blacks could be cavalry men. They were wrong: Seven black cavalry units were formed during the Civil War.[2]

After one terrible battle in Missouri, a newspaper reporter wrote, "It is useless to talk any more about Negro courage. The men fought like tigers, each and every one of them."[3]

The first all-black regiment in the Union Army was the First Louisiana Native Guards. The men showed their courage when they tried to capture Port Hudson, Louisiana, in May 1863.

The First Louisiana Native Guards arrived for duty at Fort Macombe in Louisiana. They joined the Union army in September 1862, two months after Congress gave Lincoln the power to hire black soldiers.

The Native Guards pushed on through bullets and shells all day long. Even when soldiers were badly hurt, they went back to fighting as soon as they were bandaged. But the Confederates were fierce, and finally the Native Guards

were forced to withdraw. Almost 300 African-American soldiers were dead, and more than 1,500 were badly wounded. Yet the men had proved that they were good soldiers.

The soldiers "fought like devils," wrote a white soldier from Wisconsin. "They made five charges on a battery that there was not the slightest chance of their taking, just . . . to show our boys that they *could* and *would* fight."[4]

The North fought for more than a month to take control of Port Hudson, right. They had to stop the Confederates from shipping cotton, soldiers, and supplies on the Mississippi River. African-American soldiers played a key role in one of the battles.

Only a few days later, African-American soldiers showed their courage once again. At Milliken's Bend, Louisiana, a small force of black and white soldiers was attacked by 1,500 Confederates. The black soldiers had been drilled for only a few days. They had very little idea of how to fight or how to use their weapons. Yet hundreds of them fought bravely and died in the hand-to-hand struggle.

"I have six broken bayonets to show how bravely my men fought,"

A bayonet is a knife that fits into the muzzle end of a rifle.

said Captain Matthew M. Miller, who lost half his Louisiana unit in the Union victory.[5]

~~~

I t is easy to understand why African Americans would fight for the North. Yet there were also some African Americans who joined the Confederate army. Why would black men want to fight for the South?

The battle at Milliken's Bend ended in the loss of many African-American lives.

Not all blacks in the South were slaves. Some were free men who owned property. They were afraid it would be taken away by

From the start, black soldiers were often treated badly in both the North and South. The black men in one Pennsylvania unit had stones thrown at them daily by soldiers in a white troop.[6]

The 27th U.S. Colored Infantry was organized in Ohio in January 1864. Here, the soldiers made camp near Petersburg, Virginia, months later.

Union soldiers, and so they stayed loyal to the South. Also, many slaves were frightened by stories that Northerners would treat them far worse than Southerners.[7]

Many blacks were forced to work in the Confederate army. They cooked food, carried wounded soldiers on stretchers, and built roads. The

The Confederates took some slaves from each plantation to do hard labor.[8] The slaves above made their own choice—they ran off with the Union soldiers marching by.

Confederate army needed more soldiers, too. Some—but not all—Southerners thought that black men should fight. "He [the black man] must play an important part in this war," said a Louisiana farmer. "He *caused* the fight."[9]

But by the time Confederate leaders finally agreed to enlist African Americans, the war was almost over. Few slaves joined the Confederate army.

African Americans also served bravely at sea. In the North, about 30,000 African Americans served in the U.S. Navy. This was about one-fourth of all Union sailors.[10]

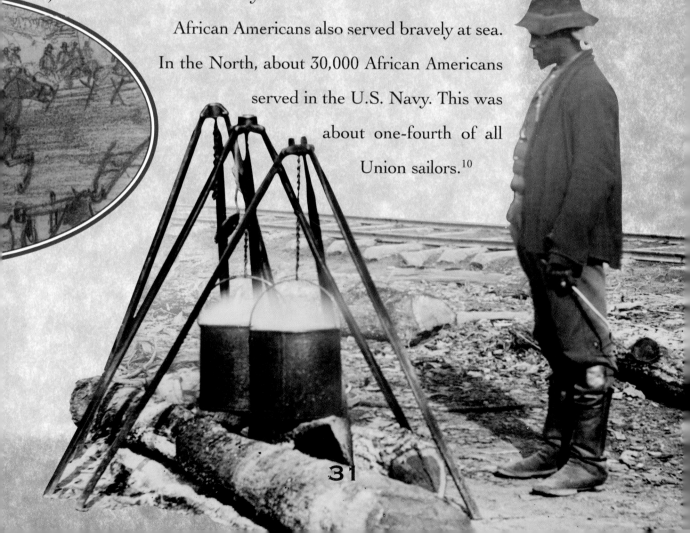

This African-American cook was preparing a meal for the soldiers of his unit.

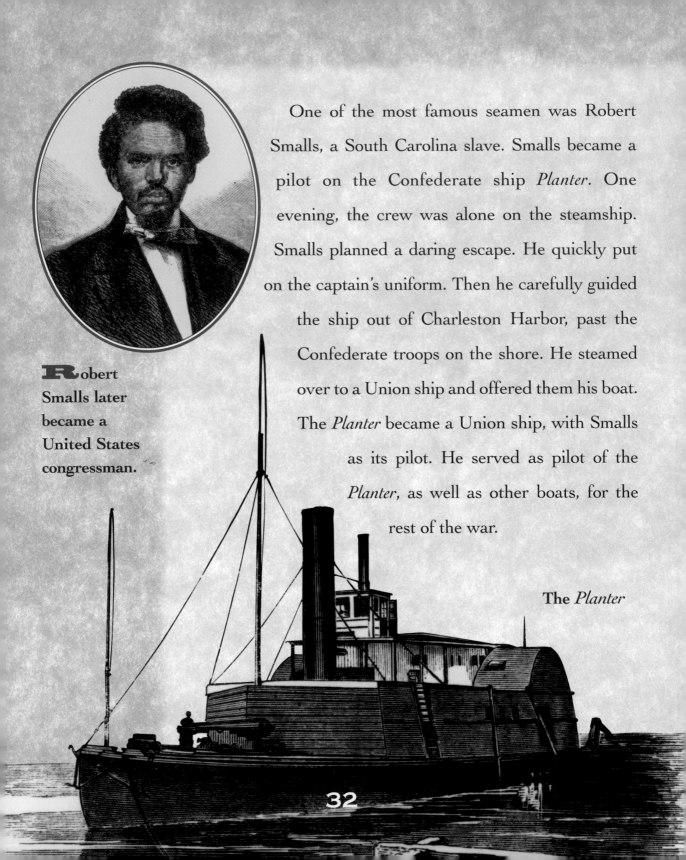

One of the most famous seamen was Robert Smalls, a South Carolina slave. Smalls became a pilot on the Confederate ship *Planter*. One evening, the crew was alone on the steamship. Smalls planned a daring escape. He quickly put on the captain's uniform. Then he carefully guided the ship out of Charleston Harbor, past the Confederate troops on the shore. He steamed over to a Union ship and offered them his boat. The *Planter* became a Union ship, with Smalls as its pilot. He served as pilot of the *Planter*, as well as other boats, for the rest of the war.

Robert Smalls later became a United States congressman.

The *Planter*

CHAPTER FIVE

SEPARATE BUT UNEQUAL

African Americans fought bravely and were praised for their courage during the Civil War. But they were not treated as equals to whites. Their days were often filled with hard jobs known as fatigue duty. They dug trenches, built roads, and unloaded supplies. Black soldiers were not able to devote their time to

African-American soldiers often did heavy work instead of fighting battles. The men above were building pens to hold prisoners of war.

drilling and preparing for battle. "Instead of the musket, it is the spade and wheelbarrow and the axe," complained one soldier in a Louisiana unit.[1]

Some soldiers became angry, saying they were still being treated like slaves. Private William G. Barcroft refused to work one day. He said he was being used as a laborer, not a soldier. Barcroft was punished for not obeying an officer. He was sentenced to two years in an army prison.

These contrabands wore old Union army uniforms and drove wagons for the soldiers.

The white soldiers drilled, headed off to battle, or rested in camp. Meanwhile, the black soldiers often worked eight to ten hours a day doing hard labor. As a result, the black soldiers were tired and poorly prepared for combat. They had worn-out uniforms and dirty guns. It is not surprising that their spirits were often low.

The officers complained until the War Department finally took action. In June 1864, a new rule said that black soldiers must not be given more fatigue duty than white soldiers. Still, this rule was often ignored.

THE FACTS ON:
SOLDIER DEATHS

◈ Twice as many African-American soldiers died from disease during the war as whites. The blacks had worn-out clothing, so they suffered more in bad weather. Also, many white doctors did not want to take care of black soldiers.[2]

Money was another sore point. White soldiers received $13 each month, plus extra money for clothing. Blacks were given only $10 per month, and $3 was subtracted for their clothing. This left the black soldier with only $7. That was about half the pay a white soldier received.

Camps for contrabands were often dirty and unhealthy.

The 5,000 black soldiers recruited by the War Department had been promised the same pay and rations as other soldiers in the Union army. When they found out that whites were getting more, black soldiers were furious. "It is a shame the way they treat us," said London S. Langley, a soldier in the Fifty-fourth Massachusetts Infantry (Colored). "Our officers tell me now that we are

36

soldiers. . . . If we were, we would get the same pay as the white men."³

Many black soldiers refused to accept their $10 paychecks. The men of the Massachusetts Fifty-fourth and Fifty-fifth said they would take no pay at all if it was less than the amount being given to white soldiers. It was not until June 1864 that the government provided equal pay for the U.S. Colored Troops.

Black soldiers fought hard in many, many battles.

About 38,000 African Americans gave their lives to the fight for freedom. Twenty-four received the Medal of Honor, right.

Black soldiers were also given harsher punishments if they were captured by the enemy. Confederates claimed they would treat captured soldiers as runaway slaves, and their officers would be executed.

One of the most brutal battles took place at Fort Pillow in Tennessee. Fifteen hundred Confederate troops attacked the fort in April 1864. It was held by 570 Union soldiers—half of them black. The Union soldiers were finally forced to drop their guns. Many raised their hands in the air to

Two brothers in uniform.

surrender. Yet the Confederates savagely shot down the Union soldiers. The killings spurred on blacks through the rest of the war with the battle cry, "Remember Fort Pillow!"

During the four years of the Civil War, African-American soldiers faced many injustices—less money, shabby uniforms, poor equipment, and the risk of being shot or enslaved if they were captured. Yet they fought with courage and loyalty.

The war ended in 1865. More than 180,000 African Americans had served in the Northern army and navy. Before the war, more than half of these men had been slaves in the South.[4]

Most African Americans went home after the war. In the North, many soldiers used the money they had earned to buy land or get training in a skill, such as bricklaying. In the South, many African Americans became field workers on or near the plantations where they had been slaves.[5] Their lives were not much different than they were before the war. But now they were sharecroppers, not slaves. They farmed the land in exchange

Drummer boy Taylor served with the 78th Regiment of the U.S. Colored Infantry.

for part of the money the crop would make at the market.

The war had ended, but the fight for equal rights for all Americans was just beginning. African Americans had little money or education. Life was not easy for them. Over the next hundred years, they would struggle to be treated as equal citizens.

There was much joy when soldiers came home safely after the war.

"If we hadn't become soldiers, all might have gone back as it was before," said Thomas Long, a former slave who joined the First South Carolina Volunteers. "But now things can never go back, because we have showed our energy and our courage."[6]

◆ EQUAL RIGHTS ◆

Laws were passed to make sure African Americans were treated more fairly. In 1865, the THIRTEENTH AMENDMENT to the U.S. Constitution put an end to slavery throughout the United States. Three years later, the FOURTEENTH AMENDMENT gave African-American citizens equal protection under the law and the right to hold a political office. In 1870, the FIFTEENTH AMENDMENT gave African-American men the right to vote.

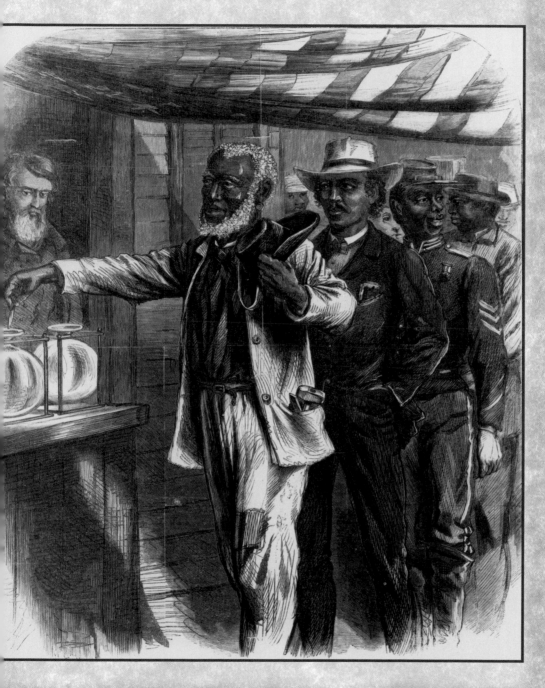

Five years after the Civil War, African-American men were given the right to vote.

AFRICAN-AMERICAN SOLDIERS ★ IN THE ★ CIVIL WAR TIMELINE

FEBRUARY 1861
Confederate States of America is formed.

APRIL 12, 1861
Fort Sumter is attacked; the Civil War begins.

ROBERT SMALLS

MAY 12, 1862
Robert Smalls makes a daring escape from the Confederacy with the steamship *Planter*.

AUGUST 1862
The War Department organizes 5,000 black volunteers to fight in the Union army.

COLOR'D MEN WANTED! Bounty, $602. Cash down, 350. Besides State, and United States pay, &c.

Pre-1860	1860	1861	1862

AUGUST 1619
First African slaves are sold in Jamestown, Virginia.

1793
The cotton gin is invented, giving new life to the slave industry in the South.

NOVEMBER 1860
Abraham Lincoln is elected president.

DECEMBER 1860
South Carolina is the first of eleven states to secede from the Union.

JULY 21, 1861
Confederacy wins the First Battle of Bull Run.

JULY 17, 1862
Congress rules that black Americans can now enlist in Union army.

SEPTEMBER 1862
Louisiana Native Guards becomes first all-black regiment to formally join Union army.

JANUARY 1, 1863
Lincoln issues the Emancipation Proclamation.

MAY 27, 1863
Native Guards attack Port Hudson, Louisiana.

APRIL 1864
Black soldiers are ruthlessly shot down by Confederates at Fort Pillow, Tennessee.

SEPTEMBER 29, 1864
Black soldiers fight heroically at Battle of New Market Heights, Virginia. Fourteen earn Medal of Honor.

MARCH 23, 1865
Confederacy issues law to use slaves as soldiers.

APRIL 9, 1865
Confederate general Robert E. Lee surrenders to Union general Ulysses S. Grant.

MAY 13, 1865
The last battle of the Civil War is fought at Palmetto Ranch, Texas.

1863 **1864** **1865**

JULY 18, 1863
The Fifty-fourth Massachusetts Regiment leads an assault on Fort Wagner, South Carolina.

JUNE 15, 1864
Congress grants equal pay for black soldiers.

OCTOBER 2, 1864
About 600 black soldiers of the Fifth and Sixth U.S. Colored Cavalry attack the salt furnaces at Saltville, Virginia. (First Battle of Saltville)

APRIL 15, 1865
Lincoln dies after being shot; Andrew Johnson becomes president.

DECEMBER 6, 1865
The Thirteenth Amendment to the Constitution abolishes slavery in the United States.

Words to Know

bayonet—A steel blade attached at the end of a rifle.

border states—States that allowed slavery, yet were part of the Union: Maryland, Delaware, Kansas, and Missouri.

civil war—A war between people of the same country.

colored/Negro—Words that were used for African Americans.

Confederate States of America—The new country formed in 1861 by the eleven Southern states that withdrew from the United States: South Carolina, Mississippi, Florida, Alabama, Georgia, Louisiana, Texas, Virginia, Arkansas, North Carolina, and Tennessee. Also called the Confederacy.

contraband—A slave who escaped during the Civil War and took refuge with the Union army.

Emancipation Proclamation—Abraham Lincoln's document that declared slaves in the rebelling states to be free.

enlist—To enroll in the armed forces.

plantation—A large farm.

ration—A set amount of food.

recruit—To enroll people as members of the armed forces.

secede—To withdraw or break away.

≈ Chapter Notes ≈

CHAPTER 1.
A New Country
1. Russell Duncan, *Where Death and Glory Meet: Robert Gould Shaw and the 54th Massachusetts Infantry* (Athens, Georgia: University of Georgia Press, 1999), p. 112.
2. Noah Andre Trudeau, *Like Men of War: Black Troops in the Civil War, 1862–1865* (Boston: Little, Brown and Co., 1998), p. 72.
3. Ervin L. Jordan, Jr., *Black Confederates and Afro-Yankees in Civil War Virginia* (Charlottesville: University Press of Virginia, 1995), p. 272.
4. Catherine Clinton, *The Black Soldier* (Boston: Houghton Mifflin Company, 2000), pp. 22–23.
5. Geoffrey C. Ward, *The Civil War: An Illustrated History* (New York: Alfred A. Knopf, Inc., 1990), p. 12.
6. African-American Civil War Soldiers, Frederick Douglass, <http://americancivilwar.com/colored/frederick_douglass/html> (June 27, 2003).
7. Dudley Taylor Cornish, *The Sable Arm: Negro Troops in the Union Army, 1861–1865* (New York: W. W. Norton & Company, Inc., 1966), p. 5.

CHAPTER 2.
The Way Is Barred
1. Hondon B. Hargrove, *Black Union Soldiers in the Civil War* (Jefferson, North Carolina: McFarland & Company, Inc., 1988), p. 44.
2. Noah Andre Trudeau, *Like Men of War: Black Troops in the Civil War, 1862–1865* (Boston: Little, Brown and Co., 1998), p. 179.
3. Catherine Clinton, *The Black Soldier* (Boston: Houghton Mifflin Company, 2000), p. 23.
4. Charles H. Wesley, *Negro Americans in the Civil War: From Slavery to Citizenship* (New York: Publishers Company, Inc., 1967), p. 147.

CHAPTER 3.
Recruitment
1. Joseph T. Glatthaar, *Forged in Battle: The Civil War Alliance of Black Soldiers and White Officers* (New York: Penguin Books, 1990), p. 3.
2. Ibid., p. 74.
3. Ibid., p. 70.
4. Camp Nelson, Kentucky, Recruitment and Training Center, <http://www.campnelson.org/history/recruitment.htm> (June 27, 2003).

5. Hondon B. Hargrove, *Black Union Soldiers in the Civil War* (Jefferson, North Carolina: McFarland & Company, Inc., 1988), p. 207.

6. Glatthaar, p. 79.

CHAPTER 4.
The First Regiments

1. Christopher Looby, editor, *The Complete Civil War Journal and Selected Letters of Thomas Wentworth Higginson.* (Chicago: University of Chicago Press, 2000), p. 249.

2. Noah Andre Trudeau, *Like Men of War: Black Troops in the Civil War, 1862–1865* (Boston: Little, Brown and Co., 1998), p. 270.

3. Dudley Taylor Cornish, *The Sable Arm: Negro Troops in the Union Army, 1861–1865* (New York: W. W. Norton, 1966) p. 77.

4. Trudeau, p. 44.

5. Hondon B. Hargrove, *Black Union Soldiers in the Civil War* (Jefferson, North Carolina: McFarland & Company, Inc., 1988), p. 146.

6. Joseph T. Glatthaar, *Forged in Battle: The Civil War Alliance of Black Soldiers and White Officers* (New York: Penguin Books, 1990), p. 196.

7. Shelby Foote, *The Civil War: A Narrative. From Red River to Appomattox* (New York: Random House, 1974), p. 753.

8. William C. Davis, *Look Away! A History of the Confederate States of America* (New York: Simon & Schuster, Inc., 2002), p. 149.

9. Geoffrey C. Ward, *The Civil War: An Illustrated History* (New York: Alfred A. Knopf, Inc., 1990), p. 253.

10. Charles H. Wesley, *Negro Americans in the Civil War: From Slavery to Citizenship* (New York: Publishers Company, Inc., 1967), p. 167.

CHAPTER 5.
Separate but Unequal

1. Joseph T. Glatthaar, *Forged in Battle: The Civil War Alliance of Black Soldiers and White Officers* (New York: Penguin Books, 1990), p. 183.

2. Geoffrey C. Ward, *The Civil War: An Illustrated History* (New York: Alfred A. Knopf, Inc., 1990), p. 252.

3. Noah Andre Trudeau, *Like Men of War: Black Troops in the Civil War, 1862–1865* (New York: Little, Brown, and Company, 1998), p. 253.

4. Versalle F. Washington, *Eagles on Their Buttons: A Black Infantry Regiment in the Civil War* (Columbia, Missouri: University of Missouri Press, 1999), p. x.

5. Trudeau, p. 463.

6. Excerpts from *Slave Narratives*, University of Houston, edited by Steven Mintz, <http://vi.uh.edu/pages/mintz/38.htm> (June 27, 2003).

Learn More

BOOKS

Brooks, Victor. *African Americans in the Civil War*.
  Philadelphia: Chelsea House Publishers, 2000.

Haskins, James. *Black, Blue, and Gray: African Americans in the Civil War*.
  New York: Simon and Schuster Books for Young Readers, 1998.

Kallen, Stuart. *The Civil War and Reconstruction*.
  Edina, Minn.: Abdo and Daughters, 2001.

Reef, Catherine. *Civil War Soldiers: African-American Soldiers*.
  Brookfield, Conn.: Twenty-first Century Books, 1993.

INTERNET ADDRESSES

Freedom Fighters: United States Colored Troops
in the Civil War.
  <http://www.coax.net/people/lwf/data.htm>

Civil War and Reconstruction:
African-American Soldiers in the Civil War.
  <http://memory.loc.gov/ammem/ndlpedu/features/timeline/
  civilwar/aasoldrs/soldiers.html>

54th Mass. Volunteer Infantry, Co. I
  <http://www.awod.com/gallery/probono/cwchas/54ma.html>

Index

Pages numbers for photographs are in **boldface** type.